Emma

The *Oxford Progressive English Readers* series provides a wide range of reading for learners of English.

Each book in the series has been written to follow the strict guidelines of a syllabus, wordlist and structure list. The texts are graded according to these guidelines; Grade 1 at a 1,400 word level, Grade 2 at a 2,100 word level, Grade 3 at a 3,100 word level, Grade 4 at a 3,700 word level and Grade 5 at a 5,000 word level.

The latest methods of text analysis, using specially designed software, ensure that readability is carefully controlled at every level. Any new words which are vital to the mood and style of the story are explained within the text, and reoccur throughout for maximum reinforcement. New language items are also clarified by attractive illustrations.

Each book has a short section containing carefully graded exercises and controlled activities, which test both global and specific understanding.

Oxford University Press

Oxford   New York
Athens   Auckland   Bangkok   Bombay
Calcutta   Cape Town   Dar es Salaam   Delhi
Florence   Hong Kong   Istanbul   Karachi
Kuala Lumpur   Madras   Madrid   Melbourne
Mexico City   Nairobi   Paris   Singapore
Taipei   Tokyo   Toronto

and associated companies in
Berlin   Ibadan

Oxford is a trade mark of Oxford University Press

This adaptation first published 1992
This impression (lowest digit)
7   9   10   8   6

© Oxford University Press 1992

All rights reserved. No part of this publication may be reproduced, stored in a retrieval system, or transmitted, in any form or by any means, without the prior permission in writing of Oxford University Press (China) Ltd. Within Hong Kong, exceptions are allowed in respect of any fair dealing for the purpose of research or private study, or criticism or review, as permitted under the Copyright Ordinance currently in force. Enquiries concerning reproduction outside these terms and in other countries should be sent to Oxford University Press (China) Ltd at the address below

This book is sold subject to the condition that it shall not, by way of trade or otherwise, be lent, re-sold, hired out or otherwise circulated without the publisher's prior consent in any form of binding or cover other than that in which it is published and without a similar condition including this condition being imposed on the subsequent purchaser

Illustrated by Cheung Chi Ping, Elinda
Syllabus designer: David Foulds
Text processing and analysis by Luxfield Consultants Ltd

ISBN 0 19 585270 2

Printed in Hong Kong
Published by Oxford University Press (China) Ltd
18/F Warwick House East, Taikoo Place, 979 King's Road,
Quarry Bay, Hong Kong

CONTENTS

1	EMMA WOODHOUSE	1
2	EMMA AND HARRIET	5
3	CHRISTMAS	12
4	EMMA AND FRANK	19
5	THE DINNER PARTY	27
6	THE DANCE	35
7	THE TEA PARTY	40
8	FRANK AND JANE	45
9	EMMA AND MR KNIGHTLEY	50
	QUESTIONS AND ACTIVITIES	54

EMMA WOODHOUSE

The matchmaker

Emma Woodhouse was pretty, clever and rich. She and her father lived in a large, beautiful house in Highbury, near London. The house was called Hartfield House. Emma was the younger daughter of Mr Woodhouse.

Emma had an elder sister, whose name was Isabella. Isabella was married. She did not live at Hartfield House. She and her husband, John, and their five small children lived in London.

Emma's mother had died when Emma was very young.

Mr Woodhouse was quite an old man. He loved Emma more than anyone in the whole world. He did not think Emma could do anything wrong.

A woman named Miss Taylor worked for Mr Woodhouse. She looked after Emma. She was Emma's teacher and her closest friend.

Miss Taylor fell in love with a man called Mr Weston. They were friends for many years. Then they decided to marry.

At last the day of Miss Taylor's wedding came. Miss Taylor left Hartfield House. She went to live in Mr Weston's house, called Randalls.

Emma and old Mr Woodhouse were left alone. No-one else lived with them in their beautiful home.

Emma was a very clever girl. Secretly, she was quite proud of herself. She thought she was cleverer than most people.

Emma believed she could change people's lives. She believed she could change people's feelings and make them like each other. She enjoyed looking for good husbands for her women friends. She also thought she could find good wives for her men friends. Emma was a matchmaker.

Emma was very pleased with herself when Miss Taylor married Mr Weston. She thought she had made these two people fall in love. She thought she had found a very good husband for her best friend.

Mr Knightley

In the evening, after Miss Taylor's wedding, a visitor came to Hartfield House. It was Mr Knightley. He had come to see Emma and her father.

Mr Knightley was the elder brother of Isabella's husband. He was an old friend of Emma and Mr Woodhouse. He often came to see them.

'Did you have a pleasant time at the wedding?' he asked Emma.

Emma smiled at Mr Knightley.

'Yes,' she answered. 'It was wonderful to see those two people together. The wedding was beautiful. Of course, my father and I will miss Miss Taylor very much. She was my closest friend and teacher for many years. Perhaps I made a mistake when I matched Miss Taylor and Mr Weston.'

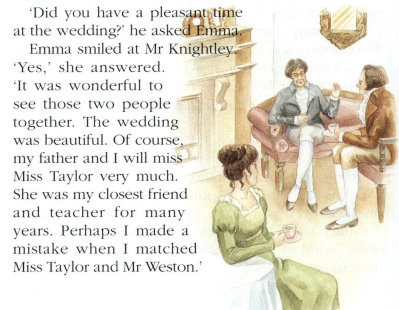

'Did you say you matched them?' asked Mr Knightley.

'Yes, I did. I was the matchmaker,' said Emma proudly.

'Oh no, Emma. Miss Taylor and Mr Weston chose each other. You did not choose for them,' said Mr Knightley with a pleasant smile.

'But I helped! I introduced them to each other. They married because I introduced them. I often invited Mr Weston to Hartfield House to visit Miss Taylor. They married because of what I did.'

'You are wrong, Emma,' said Mr Knightley.

Emma was surprised when he said this. Nobody ever told Emma Woodhouse she was wrong. That was why she always thought she was right.

Mr Knightley continued, 'When two people marry, it is because they decide to marry! Planning other people's friendships for them is dangerous, Emma.'

Soon the evening was over and Mr Knightley went home.

Emma went to her room. She was unhappy with Mr Knightley. She did not like what he had said to her. But she did not think about it any more that night. She thought about someone called Mr Elton.

Mr Elton lived in Highbury. He was the rector at the church there. Mr Elton was not married and Emma thought he should be married. She decided she would find Mr Elton a wife. As she fell asleep she thought about a wife for Mr Elton.

Harriet arrives

Miss Taylor, now Mrs Weston, often visited Emma. Emma enjoyed these visits very much.

Sometimes Mr Woodhouse invited people to visit him and Emma. Some of the people who came to see them were Mr Knightley, Mr and Mrs Weston, Mr Elton, Mrs Bates, Miss Bates and Mrs Goddard.

One evening Mrs Goddard brought a young lady named Harriet Smith to visit them.

Harriet Smith was a simple girl. She was poor. She did not have a family. She did not know who her parents were. Harriet was proud to be invited to Hartfield House.

'I will be pleasant to this poor girl,' thought Emma.

It was a happy evening. Harriet was surprised that Emma was so pleasant to her.

Emma decided to make Harriet her friend. She invited Harriet to her home again and again.

'Tell me about your life,' said Emma to Harriet one day.

'I have had a very simple life, Emma. I work at the school in Highbury. Mrs Goddard is very kind to me. I also have a friend called Mr Martin.'

'Who is Mr Martin?' asked Emma.

Harriet's face became red. 'He is a friend. I know his sisters. Mr Martin and his sisters have a farm not far from Highbury.'

Emma went home and thought about her talk with Harriet. 'I think Harriet wants to marry Mr Martin. But a farmer is not good enough for Harriet,' thought Emma. 'I know she likes him, but she should not marry him! Harriet will be a very good wife for Mr Elton.'

Emma smiled to herself. 'I will introduce them to each other. They will fall in love. Then I will arrange the marriage of Harriet to Mr Elton.'

Emma was happy to be matchmaking again.

2

EMMA AND HARRIET

A bad friendship

Mr Knightley often visited Emma's old teacher, Mrs Weston. One day he spoke to her about Emma and Harriet.

'It is not a good friendship,' said Mr Knightley.

'Why?' asked Mrs Weston.

'Emma thinks Harriet is lower than herself. She is being kind to her. That is bad for their friendship!' said Mr Knightley. 'I will tell Emma what I think.'

'Emma will not like that, Mr Knightley,' answered Mrs Weston.

'I know,' replied Mr Knightley, and he laughed. 'But if I do not say anything, Emma will make Harriet very unhappy.'

Emma was happy. She taught Harriet to dress like a lady. She combed Harriet's hair in a new way. Then she invited Mr Elton to have tea with Harriet and herself. Harriet and Mr Elton became friends. Emma watched. She felt very pleased with herself.

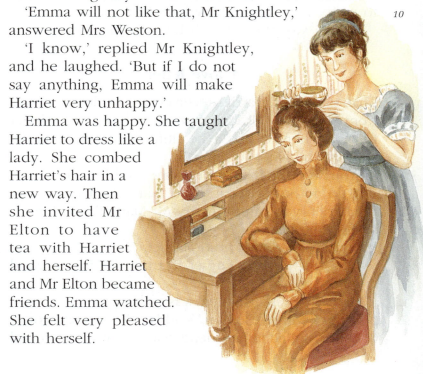

One day, Emma asked Harriet if she could draw her picture. Emma was good at drawing. She liked to draw pictures of her friends. Harriet was happy. Mr Elton was happy too. He liked Emma and Harriet. He thought Emma was very kind to draw Harriet's picture.

Mr Elton came to Emma's house every day to watch her draw Harriet. Soon the picture was finished.

'Emma, it is a beautiful picture,' said Mr Elton.

'Thank you, I am glad you like it,' said Emma.

'I will take the picture to London. I will ask someone to make a frame for it,' said Mr Elton.

Emma was happy when Mr Elton said this. 'He is taking her picture to London! That means he must love Harriet,' thought Emma. 'Soon he will ask Harriet to marry him. I just know he will!'

Emma was pleased with her matchmaking.

A love letter

That same day Harriet received a love letter. It was from Mr Martin. Mr Martin wrote to Harriet to ask her to marry him. It was a beautiful love letter. Harriet showed the letter to Emma.

'You will say "No", of course?' said Emma.

'I do not know what to do,' said Harriet.

'Harriet, you cannot marry Mr Martin!' said Emma. 'He is a farmer.'

'But he loves me,' said Harriet.

'Yes, but he is a farmer. Harriet, he is not good enough for you.'

Harriet saw that Emma was unhappy.

'Then I will refuse him,' said Harriet in a sad voice.

Emma smiled at her friend. 'Good. I was frightened

you would agree to marry him. Then I could no longer be your friend.'

'Why?' asked Harriet.

'Harriet, Mr Martin is a farmer. We do not have farmers as our friends. Farmers are not as good as we are. They are not our equals.'

'I understand,' said Harriet. 'I will not marry Mr Martin. Please help me to write a letter to him.'

Emma was happy. She helped Harriet write a letter to Mr Martin. In the letter Harriet said she refused to marry him.

Harriet was not so sure. She wanted Emma to be her friend. Harriet had never had a friend like Emma before. Emma was rich and beautiful. Emma's friendship was very important to Harriet. She did not want to make Emma angry or unhappy. She liked Mr Martin, but she sent him the letter.

The next day Mr Knightley visited Emma for tea.

'Harriet is a wonderful girl, Emma,' said he.

'Yes, she is my friend,' said Emma.

'I think Mr Martin will marry Harriet soon,' said Mr Knightley.

'He has asked her to marry him. She received a letter from him yesterday. But she has refused him,' said Emma.

'Why?' asked Mr Knightley.

'Because Mr Martin is not Harriet's equal. He is only a farmer, Mr Knightley. He is below her.'

Mr Knightley was angry. 'He is a good man and a good farmer. Harriet is a simple girl. He would be a good husband for her. He loves her and I think she loves him.'

'You are wrong, Mr Knightley!' said Emma. 'Harriet will not marry a simple farmer.'

'Emma, did you tell Harriet not to marry Mr Martin?' asked Mr Knightley in an angry voice.

'No, I did not. Harriet decided for herself. She does not want to marry a farmer.'

'Emma, are you matchmaking again?' asked Mr Knightley.

'No, I am not.' Emma's face was red.

'You will make poor Harriet unhappy, Emma,' said Mr Knightley.

Emma did not believe Mr Knightley and she told him he was silly.

Mr Knightley was very, very angry. He knew what Emma had done. He knew she had made Harriet refuse Mr Martin. He was so angry that he left Emma's house.

'Emma will break Harriet's heart,' thought Mr Knightley as he walked home. He was so angry with Emma that he did not visit her for a week.

Harriet's book of poems

Mr Elton came back from London with the drawing of Harriet. The drawing was now in a beautiful, new frame. Emma hung it on the wall. Harriet was very happy with the picture.

One day, Emma said, 'Harriet, I want you to make a book of poems.'

'I do not write poems,' said Harriet.

'No,' said Emma. 'I don't mean that you should make up poems. I mean that you should collect them.

Ask people to tell you
the poem they like best,
then write it in your book.'

'Oh, I understand. Yes, I will do that,' said Harriet.

Harriet always tried to please Emma. 'If Emma thinks I need a book of poems, then I must make one,' she thought to herself.

Emma and Harriet asked people for poems. Mr Woodhouse gave Harriet a poem. Mrs Weston also gave her one.

The next day Mr Elton visited Emma and Harriet.

'A friend wrote a poem for the book,' said Mr Elton. His face was very red. 'Here is the poem, Emma.' Then he quickly left.

The poem began with the words, 'to Miss …' But there was no name. It was a love poem. Emma read it carefully.

She looked at Harriet and said, 'I think he wrote this poem, Harriet, but he was afraid to tell you!'

Emma smiled. 'All is going well,' she thought.

Emma wrote Mr Elton's poem in Harriet's book. Secretly Emma thought it was a stupid poem. She thought Mr Elton was a silly man but good enough for Harriet.

Emma returned Mr Elton's poem to him.

'Thank you, Mr Elton. I have copied the poem into Harriet's book.'

'You did?' said Mr Elton. His face was very red. 'You wrote the poem in *Harriet's* book?'

'Yes,' said Emma, and smiled.

Harriet and Mr Elton

One day, Emma and Harriet went to see a poor family. They lived near Mr Elton's house. Emma was kind to the poor family. As Emma and Harriet left they saw Mr Elton.

'Good afternoon. What a pleasant surprise,' he said.

'Good afternoon, Mr Elton,' said the two young ladies.

'Would you like to go for a walk?' asked Mr Elton.

'I am tired,' said Emma, 'but Harriet loves walking.'

'Oh, you must come too,' said Mr Elton.

Emma said, 'I shall come with you.' But she thought to herself, 'they should be alone.' Emma stopped to tie her shoelace. As she was tying it, she broke it.

'Oh! Look what has happened. Just look at my shoelace. It's broken. Now I cannot walk with you.'

'My house is over there, Emma. We will all go and find you a new shoelace,' said Mr Elton.

Emma was disappointed. She thought she was clever to break her shoelace. But Mr Elton was so kind.

They all went to Mr Elton's house to find a new shoelace. Then they went for a walk. As they were walking, Emma thought, 'He will ask her to marry him soon. I know he loves her.'

Isabella and John arrive

Emma went home. Isabella and John and their five children arrived from London. It was Christmas. They had come to stay at Hartfield House for the holiday.

Mr Woodhouse was happy to see his elder daughter and his grandchildren. Emma was happy too. But she had less time to think about Harriet and Mr Elton. She would have to stop matchmaking for a while.

Emma thought about Mr Knightley. She did not want him to be angry with her. She invited him to dinner with the family. After dinner, they talked.

'How are you, Emma?' asked Mr Knightley.

'Well, thank you,' answered Emma.

'Are you still matchmaking?'

'Oh no!' answered Emma.

'Please let people choose for themselves, Emma,' said Mr Knightley in a pleasant voice.

Emma smiled and was quiet.

'Mr Martin is broken-hearted! He loves Harriet and he knows Harriet loves him. You stopped their marriage. Let them decide,' he repeated.

'Harriet does not love him. I do not want to talk about this any more, Mr Knightley, 'Emma said angrily.

'Very well, Emma,' said Mr Knightley in a sad voice.

Emma spoke to Isabella. Mr Knightley, Isabella's husband, John, and Mr Woodhouse all talked to one another. The family enjoyed the evening together. Then Mr Knightley went home and Emma went to bed.

'He is wrong,' thought Emma. 'I will show him he is wrong when Harriet and Mr Elton marry each other.' She smiled and fell asleep.

3

CHRISTMAS

Mr Elton and Emma

Mr and Mrs Weston invited the Woodhouse family to a Christmas Eve party at Randalls. They also invited Harriet, Mr Elton and Mr Knightley.

Harriet was ill the day before the party. Her throat hurt and she had a headache. She was very sad because she wanted to go to the party. Emma visited her with some flowers and some fruit.

As she left Harriet's house, Emma saw Mr Elton.

'How is Harriet?' asked Mr Elton.

'Not well, Mr Elton,' said Emma. 'Will you go to the party if Harriet does not go?' asked Emma.

'Yes, I will.'

'I will see you at the party then. Goodbye,' said Emma.

When Emma returned home, her brother-in-law, John, was waiting for her.

'May I speak to you, Emma?' asked John.

'Yes, John. What is wrong?'

'Emma, I believe Mr Elton is in love with you!'

Emma laughed. 'Oh, no, he is not in love with me, John. Mr Elton loves Harriet. He is going to ask her to marry him.'

'I think he loves you, Emma. Please be careful,' said John.

'John does not know Mr Elton,' thought Emma. 'He does not know that Mr Elton took Harriet's picture to London and bought a beautiful frame for it. He is wrong. Mr Elton does not love me.'

The party

That evening Emma and John gave Mr Elton a ride to the party in their carriage. It was snowing outside. Mr Elton thanked them for the ride.

They arrived at Randalls. Emma was happy to see her friend Mrs Weston. She wanted to talk to her very much. But Mr Elton came and sat next to Emma. He asked her if she was warm. He asked her if her father was well. He asked her all about her little nieces and nephews. He told her how much he liked her drawings. He would not stop talking.

Emma looked into Mr Elton's eyes. She saw that he looked very happy when he talked to her. Suddenly she thought, 'John was right! But how silly of Mr Elton to love me. He must love Harriet. I wish he would go away and talk to someone else.' But Mr Elton stayed where he was, next to Emma.

Soon it was time for dinner. Emma was happy. At the dinner table she was sitting next to Mr Weston. Mr Elton was at the other end of the table.

'Frank will be visiting us soon, Emma,' said Mr Weston. Frank Churchill was Mr Weston's son.

Many years ago Mr Weston married and had a son, Frank. Then his first wife died. Mr Weston was heartbroken. He could not look after his son alone. Frank lived with his uncle and aunt, Mr and Mrs Churchill. Frank took their name. He became Frank Weston Churchill. Many years after that Mr Weston married Miss Taylor.

Now Frank was a young man. Emma knew a lot about him. 'Perhaps he would be a good husband for me,' she thought to herself. She was very happy to hear he would come to Randalls in January.

After dinner, Mr Elton ran to sit beside Emma. Emma did not like this. She still wanted to talk to Mrs Weston.

'Harriet is so ill,' said Mr Elton. 'I am quite worried.'

'Oh, good,' thought Emma. 'He is interested in Harriet. I knew I was right!'

Emma was happy, and smiled at Mr Elton. 'I am worried too,' she said. 'I hope she gets better quickly.'

'Oh yes,' said Mr Elton, 'but I am more worried about you. I am afraid you will catch Harriet's cold.'

Emma was surprised and angry. She was so angry that she walked away from Mr Elton.

The party ends

Mr Knightley said it was snowing very hard outside. People wanted to go home before the snow was too deep. The Christmas Eve party ended quickly.

Emma rode in her carriage with Mr Elton. No-one else was with them.

They sat in the carriage. Emma did not want to talk to Mr Elton. Suddenly Mr Elton spoke.

'I love you, Emma,' cried Mr Elton. 'I love you so very much! Please be my wife.'

'Mr Elton, what is wrong with you?' said Emma in an angry voice. 'You love Harriet.'

'Harriet? No, no, no. I do not love Harriet. I love you. And I thought you loved me,' said Mr Elton.

Emma laughed. 'I do not love you, Mr Elton. I do not love you at all! I will never marry you. I thought you were in love with Harriet, not me.'

'Emma, you invited me to your home again and again. I thought you loved me.'

'Mr Elton, I invited you to my home to meet Harriet. Not me!' Emma was very surprised. Mr Elton was very sad. He was heart-broken. He got out of the carriage and walked home.

When Emma returned home she went to her bedroom. She was very sad.

'Mr Knightley was right about me,' she thought. 'I should not be a matchmaker! I should leave people alone. Poor Harriet. What have I done to her? She loved Mr Martin and I made her refuse him. I introduced her and Mr Elton. I told her that Mr Elton loved her. Now he says he wants to marry me! How could he? How could he ever think I would love a rector!' Emma was unhappy as she fell asleep.

She woke up the next day feeling better. The snow was deep outside. She could not visit Harriet. Emma promised herself she would never be a matchmaker again.

Mr Elton goes away

The Christmas holidays passed. Isabella, John and their five children returned to London.

Emma and Mr Woodhouse received a letter from Mr Elton. In the letter he said he was going to Bath to visit friends for a few weeks.

'I am surprised that Mr Elton is going away,' said Mr Woodhouse.

'Yes, I am surprised too,' said Emma. But Emma knew why Mr Elton was going away on holiday. She knew Mr Elton was broken-hearted. He wanted to go away from her.

Emma was happy Mr Elton had gone away. She did not want to see him for a long time.

Emma thought she must visit Harriet. She wanted to see how she was. Also she wanted to tell her about Mr Elton. One day she walked to Harriet's house.

'Hello, Emma,' said Harriet. 'I'm so happy to see you.'

'Hello, Harriet. How are you feeling?' asked Emma in a very sweet voice.

'I'm much better,' said Harriet. 'Emma, Mr Elton went away on holiday. Why did he do that?'

'Oh, Harriet! I must tell you what happened. I hope you will not be too angry with me.'

'Emma, you are my closest friend. I am never angry with you!'

Then Emma told Harriet about Mr Elton. She told her Mr Elton did not love her.

'I am so sorry, Harriet. I did not know he loved me. I thought he loved you.' Emma looked very sad.

'I am not angry with you, Emma. I did not love him.'

Emma was pleased when she heard that. 'Harriet is very kind,' she thought. 'I would be angry if I was Harriet.' All was well between Harriet and Emma. They were still good friends.

A letter from Frank Churchill

One day Mrs Weston visited Emma. She told Emma she had received a letter from Frank Churchill.

He said he could not come to visit them. Both Mr and Mrs Weston were very disappointed. Emma was disappointed too. She wanted to meet Frank.

Mr Knightley came for tea one afternoon.

'Mr Frank Churchill is not coming to visit us,' said Emma.

'Why not?' asked Mr Knightley.

'He said he has too much work to do,' said Emma.

'He should visit his father and step-mother,' said Mr Knightley. 'They must be very sad that he is not coming.'

'Why do you say that. Don't you like Frank?' said Emma. She did not like to hear Mr Knightly saying bad things about Frank Churchill.

'I did not say that, Emma. I said he should visit his father!' Mr Knightley smiled.

Jane Fairfax arrives

The January days passed by. One day Emma and Harriet went walking.

'We must stop and visit Mrs Bates and Miss Bates,' said Emma.

Emma did not really like going to see these ladies. Mrs Bates talked all the time. She was always talking about her niece, Jane Fairfax. Emma did not like hearing about Jane Fairfax. She did not really want to go, but Mrs Bates and Miss Bates were friends of Mr Woodhouse. Emma had to visit them sometimes.

Emma and Harriet arrived at the house where Mrs Bates and Miss Bates lived. Mrs Bates asked them to have some tea.

'I have received a letter from Jane!' said Mrs Bates. She sounded very excited.

'How nice,' said Emma. Her words were kind, but her voice was not.

'She is coming to visit us,' said Mrs Bates. 'Isn't that wonderful!'

'Wonderful!' said Emma. 'Yes, it's wonderful for you both.' She drank her tea quickly. Then she and Harriet left.

Jane Fairfax arrived a few days later. Emma went to visit her. Jane Fairfax was pretty. She was also very kind to everyone. Jane did not talk a lot. She was quiet, but she noticed other people's feelings. Also, she played the piano very well.

Emma looked at Jane. 'She is not rich,' thought Emma. 'She is pretty but she is not rich!' For a few days, Emma was pleasant to Jane.

Jane came to Hartfield House to visit Emma and her father. Emma told her about Frank Churchill.

'I have met Frank Churchill,' said Jane. 'I met him in London a few weeks ago.'

'What is he like?' asked Emma.

'Oh, he is a very pleasant man' answered Jane.

Emma waited for Jane to tell her more about Frank, but Jane did not want to talk about him. Emma was angry because she wanted to hear about Frank Churchill.

Emma played the piano. Then Jane played. She played the piano beautifully. She played far better than Emma. This made Emma angry, too.

Emma looked at Jane Fairfax. She thought, 'I do not like Jane Fairfax. I do not like Jane Fairfax at all.'

4

EMMA AND FRANK

Mr Elton is engaged

The next day Mr Knightley visited Emma.

'I have something to tell you,' said Mr Knightley. 'I do not think you will be very pleased about it.'

Just then, Jane Fairfax arrived with Miss Bates.

'Oh, Emma. Have you heard the news?' asked Miss Bates.

'No,' replied Emma.

'Mr Elton is engaged to be married!' said Miss Bates in a happy voice.

'What?' said Emma. She was very surprised.

'I was going to tell you,' said Mr Knightley.

'Who is he going to marry?' asked Emma, her face red.

'A girl from Bath,' said Miss Bates. 'He met her on his holiday and they fell in love.'

'Well, I hope they will both be very happy,' said Emma. She tried to sound kind, but her voice was not kind.

Jane Fairfax listened to all this. She thought about what she heard. She did not say anything.

It began to rain, so Miss Bates and Jane went home. Soon Mr Knightley went home, too.

Emma thought about Harriet. When the rain stopped, Harriet came to visit Emma. She looked very happy.

'Why are you so happy, Harriet?' asked Emma.

'Oh Emma, I am happy because when I was in town it started to rain and I went inside a shop.

I met Mr Martin and his sister. They were very kind to me. It was wonderful to see Mr Martin again!'

Emma was not pleased to see Harriet so happy.

'Yes, it must have been pleasant to see him,' she said. Emma looked at Harriet.

'Harriet, I have something to tell you.'

'What is it, Emma?'

'Harriet, Mr Elton is engaged to be married.'

'To whom?'

'To a girl from Bath. He met her on his holiday.'

'I hope he is very happy,' said Harriet. She smiled.

'Harriet is not unhappy about Mr Elton at all,' thought Emma. 'She likes Mr Martin.

'Harriet, you cannot marry Mr Martin,' said Emma. 'He is not good enough for you.'

Harriet looked sad. She knew she must forget about Mr Martin or Emma would be angry with her.

A visit to the Martin family

The people of Highbury were very interested in Mr Elton's young lady. Her name was Miss Hawkins. She was from a very good family and she was rich. Mr Elton was a very happy man. Emma had broken his heart but now he was happy again.

Emma and Harriet visited each other often. They had long talks together. Harriet spoke of Mr Martin and Mr Elton. Emma told Harriet she thought Mr Elton and Mr Martin were both foolish men.

One day Harriet said, 'Emma, I am going to visit the Martin family. They were very kind to me. I feel I should go and visit them at the farm very soon.'

Emma quickly said, 'Very well, Harriet. But I will go with you when you visit them.'

The next day Harriet and Emma visited Mr Martin and his sisters at their farm. They stayed for fifteen minutes. Then Emma said, 'Harriet, we must leave now.'

Harriet was very unhappy. She wanted to stay and talk longer. But she did not want Emma to be angry. Harriet and Emma left.

Emma meets Frank Churchill

On the way home they saw Mrs Weston.

'Emma,' she said, 'Frank is coming to visit us today! A surprise visit!' Mrs Weston was very happy.

'How wonderful,' said Emma.

The next day Mr and Mrs Weston and Frank Churchill arrived at Emma's home for tea. Emma met Frank. He was very pleasant young man, and good-looking, too. Emma liked him very much.

Frank drank his tea then he stood up and said, 'I met a girl called Jane Fairfax in London. Father said she is staying with Mrs Bates and Miss Bates. I must say hello to her.'

'She is a friend of mine,' said Emma, 'and she is a very pleasant young lady.' Emma watched Frank's face.

'I think he likes Jane,' she thought. She was not pleased.

The next day, Frank Churchill visited Emma again.

'Did you visit Jane Fairfax, Mr Churchill?' asked Emma in a quiet voice.

'Yes, I did,' he said. Then he was quiet.

'He will not talk to me about Jane,' thought Emma. So she changed the conversation. They talked about the weather. Then Frank left.

'I like him very much,' thought Emma. 'I do not think he likes Jane. I think he will fall in love with me.'

Jane's present

The next day Mr and Mrs Weston visited Emma.

'Where is Frank?' asked Emma.

'Frank has gone to London for a haircut!' said Mr Weston.

'For a haircut?' said Emma. She was very surprised. She thought it was strange to travel all the way to London for a haircut.

Frank returned to Highbury the next day.

Emma received a letter from the Cole family. They were neighbours. They were going to have a party at their house, and they invited Emma to come. Emma was happy. She knew Frank would go to the party.

The week passed and soon it was the evening of the party. Mr and Mrs Weston, Mr Knightley, Miss Bates, Frank Churchill, Harriet and Jane Fairfax were all there. Emma sat with Mrs Weston.

'Have you heard about Jane's present, Emma?' asked Mrs Weston.

'No. What present?' asked Emma.

'A piano,' Mrs Weston replied.

'A Piano? What piano?' asked Emma.

'Jane Fairfax received a piano. Someone sent her a new piano as a present!' said Mrs Weston.

'Who? Who sent her a piano?' asked Emma.

'Jane does not know who sent it. Some men brought it to the house this morning. They said that they did not know whom it was from!' said Mrs Weston.

Emma left Mrs Weston and went to sit with Frank Churchill. 'Did you hear about Jane's piano, Frank?' asked Emma. She watched his face very carefully.

'Yes, I heard about the piano. Do you know who sent it to her, Emma?' asked Frank.

'No,' said Emma.

Emma looked at Frank. 'He did not send Jane the piano,' she thought. 'He loves me.' Then Emma and Frank talked about other things.

Emma knows that Frank loves her

Mrs Weston came and sat with Emma and Frank.

'I think Mr Knightley sent the piano,' said Mrs Weston. Emma answered quickly. 'Oh, no,' she said. 'I am sure Mr Knightley did not send the piano.'

'Why do you say that, Emma?' asked Frank. 'Perhaps Mr Knightley did send the piano to Jane.'

'No. If Mr Knightley sent Jane the piano then he would say he sent it. He would not keep quiet about it,' said Emma.

'You are right,' said Mrs Weston. 'Mr Knightley would tell us, I am sure.'

'Well, someone sent Jane a piano,' said Frank. Then he smiled at Emma.

Emma liked Frank. She felt her face go red when he smiled at her.

'He loves me,' thought Emma, again. 'Perhaps I will love him, too.' She looked at Frank again. He was looking at Jane.

'Why are you looking at Jane?' asked Emma.

Frank's face was red. 'I do not like the way she has arranged her hair,' he said.

Emma looked at Jane. She thought Jane had arranged her hair beautifully.

Emma smiled to herself. Frank had seen something that he did not like about Jane Fairfax. Emma was very happy.

Mr Cole came to speak to Emma. 'Emma,' he asked, 'please play the piano for us.'

Emma sat at the piano and played. Frank Churchill stood by the piano and sang with Emma. Emma was happy. Everyone was watching her, and Frank was singing with her. She played and played.

'Thank you, Emma,' said Mr Cole. 'You play the piano beautifully. Now Jane, will you play the piano for us?'

'I would love to,' said Jane in a quiet voice.

Jane played the piano. Frank stood and sang with her. Everyone watched Jane and Frank. They knew Jane played the piano beautifully. And Emma knew Jane Fairfax played the piano far better than she did. Emma was angry. She was angry with Jane for playing so well. And she was angry with Frank for singing while Jane played.

Soon it was time to dance. 'I hope Frank dances with me,' said Emma to herself.

The music began.

'Emma, will you dance with me?' asked Frank Churchill.

'Yes,' said Emma. She was happy. Frank asked her to dance first.

They finished the first dance then Frank asked Emma to dance with him again, and again.

They danced and danced. Frank Churchill did not ask Jane Fairfax to dance. 'Now I know he does not like Jane at all,' thought Emma.

The party was over and Emma went home. She was so happy. She fell asleep thinking of Frank Churchill. 'Perhaps I will marry him,' she thought.

Emma and Harriet see Jane's new piano

Harriet visited Emma the next morning.

'Shall we go to the shops?' said Emma.

'Yes,' said Harriet. She wanted to please Emma. On their way to town they saw Miss Bates.

'Hello,' said Miss Bates. 'Please come to our house and see Jane's new piano.'

'How lovely,' said Emma.

Harriet and Emma arrived at the Bates' house. Jane was looking at her new piano and Frank Churchill was also there, visiting Jane and Mrs Bates.

'Play the piano, Jane,' said Frank. Jane sat at her new piano and played. This made Emma angry. But Frank came and sat with her.

'How are you today, Emma?' asked Frank. Then he and Emma talked and talked.

Emma thought, 'He told Jane to play the piano so that he could talk to me, alone.' She smiled to herself. 'Yes, he loves me very much. He is not talking to Jane at all.'

Harriet and Emma stayed with Frank, Jane, Miss Bates and Mrs Bates for the whole afternoon. Soon it was dark.

'We must go home,' said Emma to Harriet. They thanked Mrs Bates and Miss Bates, and left.

'Frank is wonderful and I love him,' Emma said to herself.

5

THE DINNER PARTY

Frank's wonderful idea

Frank Churchill loved to dance. One evening Emma and her father visited Mr and Mrs Weston.

'I think we should have a dance party!' said Frank to his father, Mr Weston.

'Where?' asked Mr Weston.

'Here, at Randalls,' said Frank with a smile.

'That would be great fun!' said Emma. She also thought Frank was wonderful and clever.

Everyone talked about the dance.

'Why don't we have it at The Crown?' asked Mr Weston. 'The Crown is a large place. Randalls is quite small for dancing, you know. There is more space at the Crown.'

The Crown was a large hotel in the centre of Highbury.

Frank and Emma thought about Mr Weston's idea. They agreed. It would be better to have the dance at the hotel.

'Let us ask Miss Bates about the dance,' said Frank.

'Why?' asked Emma. She thought Miss Bates was a very stupid woman.

'I think we should ask her,' said Frank. Then he was quiet.

Emma did not want to make Frank angry. 'All right. Let us go and ask her now,' she said.

'Good,' said Frank. Then he and Emma went in a carriage to visit Miss Bates and Jane Fairfax.

When they were there Emma watched Frank. He did not speak to Jane at all. Emma was happy.

'The dance will be great fun, Frank,' said Miss Bates 'We will all come.'

Emma and Frank returned to Randalls. Everyone helped to plan the dance at The Crown. The evening passed quickly. Then Emma and her father went home.

Emma was so happy. She talked to everyone about the dance. But Mr Knightley was not happy. He was not excited by the plan for a dance. Emma did not know why he felt this way. Harriet, Jane and Mr and Mrs Weston thought the dance would be great fun.

Is Emma in love?

One day Frank visited Emma.

'Emma,' said Frank in a sad voice. 'I have received a letter from my aunt and uncle. My aunt is very ill. I must return to London. We will arrange the dance for another time. I visited Mrs Bates, Miss Bates and Jane before I came to see you. I have told them about the dance, and I have said goodbye to them.'

'How is Jane?' Emma asked in a low voice.

'Jane is very well,' said Frank. 'Emma, I …' Frank started to speak but then his face turned very red.

'Yes, Frank?' asked Emma. 'He is going to ask me to marry him now!' she thought.

'Emma, I want to tell you something.'

'What is it?' asked Emma.

'Oh, I ... oh ...' Frank's face was red. He stood up quickly. 'I must go now. Goodbye, Emma,' said Frank very quickly.

Emma was disappointed. 'He loves me very much,' she thought. 'He will tell me he wants to marry me when he returns from London.'

Emma was sad for a week. She thought she loved Frank Churchill. She missed him very much. Emma dreamed about Frank. Sometimes she dreamed that he asked her to marry him. In her dreams she always refused Frank. That was very strange.

'I do not love him,' thought Emma. 'If I did love him I would agree to marry him in my dreams.'

A friend of happy people

Frank was away. Emma knew she did not love him, but she could not tell him about it. 'Oh, dear,' she thought, 'he loves me so very much. He is going to be sad when he asks me to marry him and I say "No". It will break his heart,' thought Emma. 'But I do not love him. I will not marry a man that I do not love.'

Emma visited Harriet. They talked about Mr Elton. He was going to be married soon. Harriet was sad.

'Why are you sad, Harriet?' asked Emma.

'I do not know why I am so sad, Emma,' answered Harriet.

Emma was angry with Harriet. 'Please be happy, Harriet. I will not be your friend if you are not happy!' said Emma. 'And I will not visit you!'

'Oh, Emma, I'm sorry. I will be happy all the time,' said poor Harriet. She smiled at Emma, but she was not really happy. 'Please, please, Emma. I will be happy!' she said.

Emma knew Harriet was not telling the truth. She knew Harriet was unhappy about Mr Elton and Mr Martin. But Emma wanted to be with happy people.

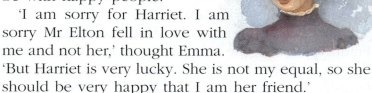

'I am sorry for Harriet. I am sorry Mr Elton fell in love with me and not her,' thought Emma. 'But Harriet is very lucky. She is not my equal, so she should be very happy that I am her friend.'

Mrs Elton

In a few weeks Mr Elton was married. One day after the wedding, Emma visited Harriet again.

'We must visit the new Mrs Elton, Harriet,' said Emma. 'Let us go this afternoon.'

'Yes,' said Harriet. She did not want to visit Mrs Elton. She went with Emma to please her.

Mr Elton was at home with his new wife when Harriet and Emma arrived. He did not appear to be very happy.

The women talked for a few minutes then Emma and Harriet left quickly.

'Mrs Elton is pretty and clever,' said Harriet in a pleasant voice.

'Oh, Harriet, Mrs Elton talks too much and she is not very pretty.'

The following week Mrs Elton visited Emma and her father. Emma did not like Mrs Elton. She thought Mrs Elton talked too much about herself.

'He has married a very silly woman,' thought Emma. 'I was right about Mr Elton. He should have married Harriet!'

Mrs Elton and Jane Fairfax

Emma's friends liked Mrs Elton, and Mr Elton loved Mrs Elton very much, of course. But Mrs Elton did not like Emma, and she did not like Harriet.

Mrs Elton was very pleased with herself. She was married to Mr Elton, the Rector of Highbury church. She thought she must be a very important person in the town.

Mrs Elton liked Jane Fairfax very much. She wanted to help her. Jane Fairfax liked Mrs Elton too.

Everyone was surprised. Mrs Weston thought Jane visited Mrs Elton to get away from Mrs Bates and Miss Bates. Emma thought Jane liked Mrs Elton because Mrs Elton was kind to her. Mr Knightley had his own ideas about Jane Fairfax and Mrs Elton.

One day Mr Knightley was visiting Emma and her father. Emma asked him about Jane Fairfax and Mrs Elton.

'Did you know that Jane Fairfax and the new Mrs Elton are friends, Mr Knightley?' she said.

'Yes, I think Mrs Elton is very kind to Jane,' answered Mr Knightley.

'Kind! Oh, Mr Knightley, Mrs Elton is a silly person. She talks too much, and Jane Fairfax is quite cold-hearted.' Emma spoke quickly.

'Jane Fairfax is a wonderful girl, Emma' said Mr Knightley.

Emma was angry. She looked at Mr Knightley. 'Do you like her a lot, Mr Knightley?'

'Oh, Emma. You are sometimes very unkind! Mrs Elton does talk a lot but she is kind to Jane. You are not kind to her!' Mr Knightley's face was very red. 'Yes,' he continued, 'I like Jane Fairfax. Many people like her. And now I am going home.' He stood up and left. He was angry with Emma.

Emma knew Mr Knightley was angry with her. She felt unhappy. Soon Mrs Weston arrived.

'Emma, do you think Mr Knightley loves Jane Fairfax?' Mrs Weston asked.

'No!' said Emma quickly. Then Mrs Weston went home.

Emma thought about what Mr Knightley had said. 'It isn't true! I am not unkind,' she thought to herself. 'I will have a dinner party for Mr and Mrs Elton. Then Mr Knightley will not be so angry with me.'

Emma planned the dinner party. She invited her sister Isabella and John. They said they would come. Mr and Mrs Elton also said 'yes', and so did Mr and Mrs Weston, Mr Knightley and Jane Fairfax. Harriet said she would not come. She did not want to be with Mr and Mrs Elton.

Emma tries to be kind

At the dinner party Jane Fairfax sat next to John. They talked and talked. John talked about handwriting.

'Some people have very good handwriting,' said Emma.

'Who?' asked Jane.

'Frank Churchill has beautiful handwriting,' said Emma.

Jane Fairfax was very quiet. The other people talked about handwriting, but Jane was silent for a long time.

After dinner the ladies sat together. Mrs Elton sat with Jane.

'Jane, you play the piano so well,' said Mrs Elton.

'Yes, you do,' said Emma. She did not want to say that to Jane but she was trying to be kind to her.

'Thank you,' said Jane.

'I'm so happy you have a new piano to play,' said Mrs Elton. 'Do you know yet who sent it?'

'No,' said Jane, quickly. But Emma saw Jane's face. She thought, 'I think she does know who gave her the piano.' But Emma said nothing.

Frank will come back soon

Mrs Weston said, 'We received a letter from Frank today.'

'Oh, what does the letter say?' asked Emma. 'How is Frank's aunt?'

'His aunt is feeling much better. And Frank is coming to visit us again,' said Mrs Weston in a happy voice.

'Oh, good,' said Emma. But she thought, 'Oh, no! He will ask me to marry him and I will break his heart!'

Mrs Elton talked and talked to Jane Fairfax. Mr Knightley was quite quiet. He was watching Emma.

Emma said, 'Jane, please play the piano.'

Jane agreed. She played the piano and everyone sang.

Emma was pleased with herself. She was kind to Mr and Mrs Elton. She was kind to Jane. She knew that Mr Knightley was pleased with her. It was a wonderful dinner party.

Later, when everyone had gone home, Emma went to her room. 'I was kind to everyone,' she thought to herself. 'I did not want Jane to play the piano but I asked her! And Mr Knightley was watching me. Now he will say I am a kind person.'

'But I still think that Mrs Elton talks too much,' she added. Then she fell asleep.

6

THE DANCE

Emma's plan

Emma knew she did not love Frank Churchill. 'But I know he loves me. What can I do? If he asks me to marry him, I must refuse. Then I will break his heart.'

Then she had an idea. 'I will not let him ask me to marry him!' she thought. 'If he doesn't ask me, I cannot refuse. He will never know that I do not want to marry him.'

Frank arrived for his stay with Mr and Mrs Weston. The next morning he visited Emma.

'Emma, we must plan the dance at the Crown,' said Frank.

'Oh, yes,' said Emma.

Frank and Emma talked about the music and the food for the dance. Then they told their friends their plans. Everyone was happy about the dance. All the young women bought new dresses.

On the night of the dance, Harriet and Emma arrived early at the Crown. Frank was there with Mr and Mrs Weston.

'You look very pretty, Emma,' said Frank. 'You look pretty too, Harriet.'

'Thank you,' said Emma and Harriet.

Mr and Mrs Elton arrived. Then Miss Bates and Jane Fairfax came in. Miss Bates talked to everyone. Mrs Elton stood with Jane. They were very glad to see each other. Frank stood with Emma. Mr Knightley arrived and talked to the other men.

The dancing started. Emma was angry because Mr Knightley would not dance with anyone. He stayed and talked to the older gentlemen.

Then Emma saw that Harriet was not dancing. She also saw that Mr Elton was not dancing. She walked over to Mr Elton.

'Hello, Mr Elton. Will you please dance with Harriet?' asked Emma.

'No! I will not!' said Mr Elton in an angry voice. 'I will not dance with Harriet!' He was very angry and his voice was very loud.

Harriet heard Emma and Mr Elton talking about her. She was very unhappy.

Mr Knightley dances

Mr Knightley watched Emma, Mr Elton and Harriet. He walked over to Harriet.

'Harriet, will you please dance with me?' said Mr Knightley in a kind voice.

'Yes, thank you,' said Harriet.

Emma was very happy now that Mr Knightley was dancing. She knew Harriet was happy, too.

Soon the music stopped. It was time for dinner. Mr Knightley waited for Emma.

'Emma, why are you such enemies with Mr and Mrs Elton?' asked Mr Knightley in a pleasant voice.

'What are you talking about, Mr Knightley?' asked Emma. Her face was red.

'I think I know why you are enemies. I think Mr Elton wanted you to marry him, not Harriet. You refused. Then Mr Elton went to Bath and met Mrs Elton on his holiday. I think Harriet and Mrs Elton also know all about this.'

A bad matchmaker

Emma could not lie to Mr Knightley. 'You are right, Mr Knightley. I was wrong about Mr Elton. I did not listen to you. I know now that you were right. I am a bad matchmaker!'

It was the first time Emma had ever said she was wrong.

Mr Knightley was very happy with Emma because of this.

'Well, Emma, Mr Elton should have married Harriet. Harriet is a wonderful girl.'

Emma smiled at him.

After dinner Mr Knightley asked Emma to dance with him. Emma liked dancing with Mr Knightley. It was a happy evening.

Frank saves Harriet

The next day something very surprising happened. Frank Churchill came to Emma's house. He was carrying Harriet in his arms.

Emma was surprised.

Harriet's face was very white. She looked quite ill. Her body was shaking, her dress was torn. Her face, hands and clothes were dirty.

'What has happened, Harriet?' asked Emma.

Harriet tried to speak. 'There were some strange men on the road. They started to attack me. But Mr Churchill came along and saved me.'

Harriet looked at Frank. 'Thank you. Oh thank you, Mr Churchill,' she said. Then Harriet started to cry very quietly to herself.

'I was happy to help you, Harriet,' said Frank with a smile.

'Come and sit down and have some tea,' said Emma to Frank and Harriet. 'And Harriet, you must wash and change. I shall give you one of my new dresses to wear. How lucky that you are the same size as me.'

Another match

They sat and drank their tea. Harriet told Emma about the men. Frank was quiet. He listened to Harriet's story.

Emma watched Harriet and Frank.

'Harriet is safe. Frank Churchill has saved her life. He was very kind to her,' thought Emma. She smiled to herself. 'Oh, I think Frank and Harriet would be a wonderful match. They should be husband and wife! I can arrange it. I know I can.'

She looked at Harriet. She looked at Frank. 'Yes,' she thought, 'they must marry each other. I know matchmaking is dangerous, but I know Harriet and I know Frank. Frank will marry Harriet, I am sure. I will arrange it.'

7

THE TEA PARTY

Frank Churchill and Jane Fairfax

One evening Emma invited Mr Knightley, Mr and Mrs Weston, Frank Churchill and Jane Fairfax to Hartfield House.

'Let's play some word-games,' said Emma.

Everyone agreed to play word-games. Each person chose different words to use in the games.

Emma used words in the game that made Jane Fairfax feel unhappy. She used words like 'piano' and 'present'.

Jane knew that Emma was being unkind to her. Her face went red. Emma laughed.

When everyone else had gone home, Mr Knightley spoke to Emma.

'Emma, why are you so unkind to Jane Fairfax?' asked Mr Knightley.

'It was just a game,' said Emma with a smile. But she knew she had been unkind to Jane.

'Emma, you must be kinder to your friends!' said Mr Knightley.

'Yes,' said Emma in a quiet voice.

Mr Knightley changed the conversation. 'Emma, I think Mr Churchill and Jane Fairfax are in love with each other. But they are hiding their love.'

'No, they aren't! You are quite wrong, Mr Knightley. Frank does not love Jane Fairfax,' said Emma crossly. 'I know Frank is not in love with Jane.' Then she was very quiet.

Mr Knightley said goodbye and went home.

Mr Knightley's beautiful gardens

A few days later Mr Knightley invited Emma to his home for a tea party. Mr Knightley's house had beautiful gardens all round it. In the gardens there were lovely flowers, tall trees, and ponds with goldfish in them. He invited everyone to walk around and look at his gardens.

Emma arrived at Mr Knightley's house. 'What a beautiful house,' she said. Everyone agreed with Emma.

Mr Knightley showed his friends around the gardens.

'These are my flower gardens,' said Mr Knightley. 'And over there you can see the vegetable gardens.'

'Oh, I know all about vegetable gardens,' said Mrs Elton. Then she talked about vegetables for a long time.

'Why is Jane so sad?'

Everyone walked along. Suddenly, Harriet stopped. She looked away from the group. Emma saw Harriet looking the other way.

'What are you looking at, Harriet?' said Emma.

'Oh, Emma, the house over there. It is Mr Martin's house. I can see the farm, too.'

Emma was angry. 'Oh, stop it, Harriet. Do not think about Mr Martin!'

Soon it was time for tea. Everyone ate, then they walked around the gardens again.

Frank Churchill had not come, and Jane Fairfax looked very sad. Emma watched Mr Knightley speak to Jane. 'Why is Jane so sad?' Emma asked herself.

Suddenly, Jane went home. Then Frank Churchill arrived. He said something had happened to him on the way to Mr Knightley's house. It had made him late.

Emma took Harriet by the arm and they walked around the goldfish ponds with Frank. 'He is smiling at Harriet. Good,' thought Emma.

The picnic

A few days later, Emma planned a picnic. She asked her friends to go to a place called Box Hill.

The Tea Party

The weather was good so everyone wanted to go.

At the right time they all arrived at Box Hill.

'Our picnic will be great fun,' said Emma.

On the way to the picnic place Mr and Mrs Elton walked alone. Emma walked with Harriet and Frank. Mr Knightley walked with Miss Bates and Jane Fairfax. At the top of the hill they found a lovely place for the picnic. They all sat down on the grass.

'Everyone is very quiet,' said Emma with a smile. 'Frank, you and I are the only people talking!'

'You are right, Emma,' said Frank in a loud voice. 'I think everyone should tell us what they are thinking!'

'Oh, yes. Everyone must say what they are thinking!' said Emma.

'Oh, but I never know what I am thinking!' said Miss Bates.

'I am not surprised,' said Emma in an unkind voice. Emma did not like Miss Bates.

Miss Bates' face went red. Her feelings were hurt. But Emma laughed.

Jane Fairfax is leaving

Mr Knightley was angry with Emma. Everyone was silent again. Then Mrs Weston changed the conversation. But the group was not happy.

'I am going home,' said Mrs Elton. The others quickly agreed with her.

'Emma, I want to speak to you,' said Mr Knightley.

'I know I was unkind, Mr Knightley,' said Emma. 'But Miss Bates talks so much, and she never says anything interesting.'

'You are very unkind sometimes,' said Mr Knightley in an angry voice. Then he turned and walked away.

Emma was surprised. She felt very sad, too. 'Oh, I do not want Mr Knightley to be angry with me again,' she thought.

Emma ran to find Harriet. They rode home in a carriage without speaking. 'I will be kinder to people, I promise,' Emma said to herself.

The next day Emma went to see Miss Bates.

'Oh, Emma, Jane Fairfax is leaving,' said Miss Bates.

'Where is she going?' asked Emma in surprise. 'She has a job in London,' said Miss Bates.

'There is something wrong,' thought Emma. Emma stayed and talked to Miss Bates for a long time. She was very kind to her. But she thought of Jane. 'Yes, something is wrong,' she said to herself.

8

FRANK AND JANE

Sad news

When Emma returned to her home, she found that Mr Knightley had come to see her.

'I have been visiting Miss Bates,' said Emma. She looked at Mr Knightley. 'I wanted to tell her I was sorry for what I said.'

'I am glad to hear that, Emma,' said Mr Knightley.

Emma was very happy. She knew Mr Knightley was pleased with her.

Mr Knightley explained that he was going to London for a few days. He had some work to do there. Emma was sad that he was leaving.

The next day Mrs Weston came to tea.

'Oh, Emma, we have had sad news. Frank Churchill's aunt has died suddenly in London,' said Mrs Weston.

'That is very sad news,' said Emma. 'I will tell Harriet.'

Emma on her own

Emma sat and thought about her friends. Jane Fairfax had left, and was working in London. Mr Knightley was working in London, too. Frank Churchill was away because his aunt had died. Emma was sad because she was by herself so much. So many of her friends were away.

The week passed. Then, one day, Mr Weston came to see Emma.

'Emma, please come home with me. Mrs Weston must talk to you,' said Mr Weston. 'Please come now!'

Emma went quickly to see Mrs Weston.

'What is it? What is wrong?' Emma asked Mrs Weston.

'Oh, Emma, I have something to tell you,' said Mrs Weston. 'I hope you will not be angry or sad.'

'What is it? What has happened?' said Emma quickly.

'Frank came to visit us today. He told us he is engaged to marry Jane Fairfax,' said Mrs Weston.

'Jane Fairfax! When?'

'They have been secretly engaged for months,' said Mrs Weston.

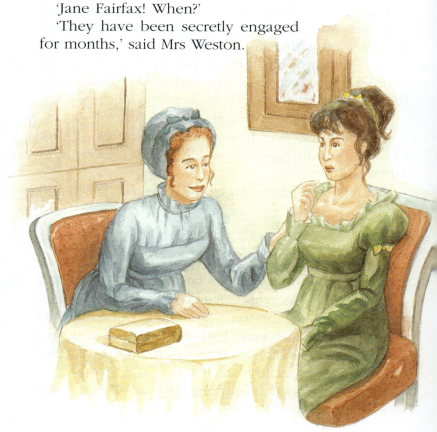

'What will I tell Harriet?'

Emma was very surprised. She thought of Harriet.

'Emma, I hope you are not in love with Frank,' said Mrs Weston.

'No, I am not in love with him. A few months ago I thought I loved him. But I know now I did not love him,' said Emma.

'I am very happy to hear that,' said Mrs Weston.

'I hope Frank and Jane will be very happy,' said Emma. But she thought of Harriet. She left and returned home.

'What will I tell Harriet?' thought Emma. 'I have chosen two men for her. Mr Elton did not love her, and now Frank doesn't love her. Harriet will be so angry with me.' Emma was sad and frightened.

A few hours later Harriet visited Emma.

'Oh, Emma, have you heard about Jane and Frank Churchill?' asked Harriet. She was smiling.

'Yes,' said Emma as she watched Harriet's face.

'It is wonderful news. I hope they will be happy,' said Harriet.

Emma is in love

Emma did not understand

'Harriet, why are you happy? I thought you liked Frank Churchill?' asked Emma.

'No, Emma, I do not like Frank. I love someone else,' said Harriet with a smile.

'Who?' asked Emma.

'Mr Knightley!' said Harriet.

'Mr Knightley!' said Emma in a surprised voice. 'Oh, you love Mr Knightley?'

'Yes,' said Harriet.

Emma was very quiet. 'Harriet, I am very tired. Please go home, now. I will see you again soon.'

Emma was alone. She did not know what to think. 'She cannot love Mr Knightley. She will not marry him,' Emma said to herself. Emma was very sad. 'He danced with her at The Crown. Mr Knightley is very kind to Harriet. But he will not marry her.'

Suddenly, Emma understood why Mr Knightley could not marry Harriet or anyone else. 'I love Mr Knightley. I, Emma Woodhouse, love Mr Knightley and I want to marry him.'

Emma needs time to think

Emma was surprised by her feelings. 'But Mr Knightley thinks I am unkind to people. He does not love me. I must make him love me. I will make my own match!'

'And I have been unkind to poor Harriet. Mr Knightley was right. I have broken Harriet's heart first with Mr Martin then with Mr Elton. Now I will break her heart with Mr Knightley. Oh, I am such a bad friend.' Emma felt very unhappy.

The next day Emma wrote a letter to Harriet. She told Harriet not to visit her for a few days. Emma needed time to think.

Mrs Weston visited her one day. 'Emma, Jane Fairfax came to see me yesterday. She asked me to tell you something.'

'What did she say?' asked Emma.

'She said she wanted to be your friend. She wanted to thank you because you were always so kind to her.'

Emma was surprised. 'That was very kind of Jane.'
Emma remembered all the bad things she had done and said. She knew she had been very unkind to Jane.

'Mr Knightley was right about Jane, too,' thought Emma. 'Oh, I love him so very much. Perhaps he will marry Harriet. Then I will be broken-hearted!'

9
EMMA AND MR KNIGHTLEY

Emma cries

The next day Emma went for a walk alone. She heard someone behind her. It was Mr Knightley.

'Oh, Mr Knightley, you surprised me!' said Emma. She was happy to see him. But she was frightened he would speak to her about Harriet.

'Hello, Emma. Are you very sad?' asked Mr Knightley.

'Sad? About what?' asked Emma.

'Are you sad about Frank Churchill and Jane Fairfax?'

'Mr Knightley, I am very happy for Frank and Jane. Why should I be sad?'

'I thought you loved Frank and wanted to marry him!' said Mr Knightley. He watched Emma's face.

'I? Love Frank? Oh, no, Mr Knightley, I do not love Frank.' Emma watched Mr Knightley's face.

'I am happy to hear that,' said Mr Knightley.

'Emma, there is something I want to speak to you about,' said Mr Knightley.

Emma was frightened. 'He will break my heart,' she thought.

'Is it about Harriet?' asked Emma. 'Do you want to speak to me about Harriet?'

'Harriet? What do you mean, Emma?' said Mr Knightley.

'You love Harriet and you want to marry her. Is that right?' asked Emma. She was almost crying.

'Emma, I do not love Harriet. I love you!' said Mr Knightley. 'I have always loved you, Emma. Will you marry me?'
'Oh, Mr Knightley, I love you, too.' Then Emma cried and cried. 'Yes, I will marry you.'
'We will be very happy together, Emma,' said Mr Knightley.

Wedding plans

'I love you,' said Emma again. 'You tell me the truth about myself. You are so kind to people. I have learned so much from you. I have learned to let people choose for themselves. I have been so unkind to Jane and to Harriet. Harriet will hate me.' Emma was speaking very quickly until she said Harriet's name.

'Oh, Mr Knightley, Harriet loves you, now.'

'Oh, no,' said Mr Knightley. 'Emma, I told you to let Harriet marry Mr Martin. They loved each other. And now you have told Harriet to love me. She will be sad, again. Oh, Emma … no more matchmaking for you … ever!'

Emma laughed. She was so happy. 'You are right!'

Emma and Mr Knightley walked to her house. Emma knew her father did not want her to marry while he was alive. But she wanted to marry Mr Knightley soon. They drank tea with Mr Woodhouse but they did not tell him of their plans.

Mr Knightley went home. Emma was alone. She thought of Harriet. 'I am so very happy for the first time in my life. But Harriet will hate me. And she will be broken-hearted again.'

The next day Mr Knightley visited Emma.

'Emma, I love you. We must marry soon,' said Mr Knightley.

'But my father is alive. I must stay with him. I must take care of him,' said Emma.

'Emma, you do not have to leave him,' said Mr Knightley. 'We will live with him at Hartfield House for a while.'

'Oh, that would be wonderful,' said Emma. 'Now we can speak to him about a wedding.' She was very happy. She knew her father would be happy if she and Mr Knightley lived with him.

'I am going to tell him soon,' said Mr Knightley. Then he said goodbye to Emma and went home.

The best matchmaker of all

Emma did not want to see Harriet. She wrote her a letter and told her what had happened.

After a few days she received a letter from Harriet. It was not an angry letter, but Harriet said she did not want to see Emma for a long time.

Emma understood. She wrote back to Harriet and told her she understood her feelings. Perhaps one day they would be friends again.

Mr Knightley spoke to Mr Woodhouse about marrying Emma. At first Mr Woodhouse was not very happy. Mr Knightley said that he and Emma would live with Mr Woodhouse at Hartfield House. Then, Mr Woodhouse agreed that Mr Knightley and Emma could marry.

Everybody was very happy. Mr and Mrs Weston, Mrs Bates and Miss Bates, Frank Churchill and Jane were all happy for Emma and Mr Knightley.

Then the news came that Harriet and Mr Martin were engaged to be married. Emma was surprised.

'I do not know why you are so surprised,' said Mr Knightley. 'I told you Harriet should marry Mr Martin months ago.' He smiled at Emma.

'Everyone is happy now,' said Emma. 'You were right. Harriet will be happy with Mr Martin. Then Harriet and I will be friends again. I think, Mr Knightley, that you are the best matchmaker of all!' They laughed together.

QUESTIONS AND ACTIVITIES

CHAPTER 1

Put the notes about these people in the right boxes.

	PERSON		NOTES
1	Emma Woodhouse	(a)	A simple, poor girl with no family of her own.
2	Mr Woodhouse	(b)	A farmer.
3	Mr Knightley	(c)	The rector of the church at Highbury.
4	Mr Elton	(d)	Father of Isabella and Emma.
5	Harriet Smith	(e)	Thinks she is cleverer than most people.
6	Mr Martin	(f)	His younger brother is married to Emma's sister.

CHAPTER 2

Put the beginnings of these sentences with the right endings.

1. Emma taught Harriet to dress like a lady,
2. Mr Elton became friends with Harriet,
3. Mr Elton took Harriet's picture to London,
4. Emma thought Mr Elton loved Harriet,

(a) ... and she thought he would ask Harriet to marry him.
(b) ... and she combed Harriet's hair in a new way.
(c) ... so she refused to marry Mr Martin.
(d) ... so Emma felt very pleased with herself.

5	Mr Martin asked Harriet to marry him,	(e)	... because he wanted to have a frame made for it.
6	Harriet did not want to make Emma angry,	(f)	... but Emma said a farmer was not right for her.

CHAPTER 3

The underlined sentences are all in the wrong paragraphs. Which paragraph should they go in? Write them out in the right place.

1 Harriet was ill and Emma visited her. <u>Mr Elton told Emma he loved her and asked her to marry him.</u> Mr Elton told her that he would go to the party.
2 John told Emma that he thought Mr Elton was in love with her. <u>Outside Harriet's house she met Mr Elton.</u> She thought Mr Elton loved Harriet.
3 At the party Mr Elton could not stop talking to Emma. <u>He got out of the carriage and walked home.</u> This was only because he was afraid that Emma would catch it.
4 Emma rode home in her carriage with Mr Elton. <u>He told her he was worried about Harriet's c old.</u> Emma said she did no love him and would never marry him.
5 Mr Elton was broken-hearted. <u>Emma did not believe it.</u> Emma promised herself she would never be a matchmaker again.

CHAPTER 4

Put these names in the right gaps. You may have to use some more than once: ***Jane, Frank, Emma, Mr Knightley, Mrs Weston.***

At the Coles' party everyone was talking about (1) ____'s present. Someone had sent her a piano, but no one knew who. (2) ____ asked Emma if she knew, but she didn't. (3) ____ thought Frank could not have sent it. She was sure that (4) ____ loved her, not Jane. (5) ____ thought (6) ____ had sent the piano, but Emma said that he would not keep quiet about it if he had.

Chapter 5

Fill the gaps using each word once to say what this part of the story is about: **tell, fun, returned, aunt, face, dance, marry, another, wonderful.**

Frank wanted to have a (1) ____ party. Emma thought that would be great (2) ____. She thought Frank was (3) ____.

Then Frank had to go to London because his (4) ____ was ill. The dance would have to be arranged for (5) ____ time. Before he left Frank wanted to (6) ____ Emma something. His (7) ____ went red, but he just said he had to go. Emma thought Frank would tell her he wanted to (8) ____ her when he (9) ____.

Chapter 6

There is something wrong in the underlined part of all these sentences: correct them to say what happened.

1 At the dance Emma was angry <u>because Mr Knightley would not sing</u>.
2 She saw that <u>Harriet and Mr Weston</u> were not dancing.
3 Emma asked Mr Elton <u>to dance with Miss Bates</u>.
4 <u>Mr Elton said quietly</u> that he would not dance with Harriet.
5 Mr Knightley <u>asked Emma to dance with him</u>.

Chapter 7

Copy the table and write the answers in their correct places. The name of the house where Emma lives will appear in the centre of the table. Choose from: **Box, grass, vegetable, Martin, knew, goldfish, quiet, gardens, tea, showed, hill, surprised, feelings, picnic.**

At the (1) ____ party Mr Knightley (2) ____ everyone around his (3) ____. There were lovely flowers, tall trees, and ponds with (4) ____ in them. There were also some (5) ____ gardens. Harriet could see a farm from Mr Knightley's gardens. It was Mr (6) ____'s farm. Emma was angry. She did not like Harriet thinking about him.

Emma asked her friends to go to (7) _____ Hill for a (8) _____. They found a lovely place at the top of the (9) _____, and they all sat down on the (10) _____. Everyone was very (11) _____. Frank said everyone should say what they were thinking. Miss Bates said she never (12) _____ what she was thinking and Emma said that she was not (13) _____. Miss Bates's (14) _____ were hurt.

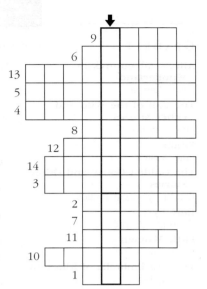

CHAPTER 8

Some of these statements are true, but others are false. Which are the true ones?

1. Mrs Weston told Emma that Frank was engaged to marry Jane.
2. Emma knew that she loved Frank.
3. Emma thought Jane Fairfax would be angry with her.
4. Harriet thought the news about Frank and Jane was wonderful.
5. She was not angry because she loved someone else.
6. Harriet told Emma that she loved Mr Martin.
7. Emma wanted to marry Mr Knightley herself.

CHAPTER 9

*Who did these things: **Mr Knightley**, **Emma**, **Mr Woodhouse**, or **Harriet**?*

1. Who told Emma he loved her, and asked her to marry him?
2. Who told Mr Knightley that Harriet loved him?
3. Who said that there must be no more matchmaking?
4. Who did not want Emma to get married?
5. Who said that he and Emma would live at Hartfield House?
6. Who was engaged to Mr Martin?

GRADE 1

Alice's Adventures in Wonderland
Lewis Carroll

The Call of the Wild and Other Stories
Jack London

Emma
Jane Austen

The Golden Goose and Other Stories
Retold by David Foulds

Jane Eyre
Charlotte Brontë

Little Women
Louisa M. Alcott

The Lost Umbrella of Kim Chu
Eleanor Estes

Tales From the Arabian Nights
Edited by David Foulds

Treasure Island
Robert Louis Stevenson

GRADE 2

The Adventures of Sherlock Holmes
Sir Arthur Conan Doyle

A Christmas Carol
Charles Dickens

The Dagger and Wings and Other Father Brown Stories
G.K. Chesterton

The Flying Heads and Other Strange Stories
Edited by David Foulds

The Golden Touch and Other Stories
Edited by David Foulds

Gulliver's Travels — A Voyage to Lilliput
Jonathan Swift

The Jungle Book
Rudyard Kipling

Life Without Katy and Other Stories
O. Henry

Lord Jim
Joseph Conrad

A Midsummer Night's Dream and Other Stories from Shakespeare's Plays
Edited by David Foulds

Oliver Twist
Charles Dickens

The Prince and the Pauper
Mark Twain

The Stone Junk and Other Stories
D.H. Howe

Stories from Shakespeare's Comedies
Retold by Katherine Mattock

The Talking Tree and Other Stories
David McRobbie

Through the Looking Glass
Lewis Carroll

GRADE 3

The Adventures of Tom Sawyer
Mark Twain

Around the World in Eighty Days
Jules Verne

The Canterville Ghost and Other Stories
Oscar Wilde

David Copperfield
Charles Dickens

Fog and Other Stories
Bill Lowe

Further Adventures of Sherlock Holmes
Sir Arthur Conan Doyle

Great Expectations
Charles Dickens